Wild Butterfly: Finding Your True North

ISBN 978-9914-742-20-6

For permission requests, contact the author with the subject line "Attention: Permissions Request" addressed to wayua.naomi@yahoo.com or nwayua2016@gmail.com

Book layout: *Kizuribooks Publishers.*

To Wendy,
thank you for
being an inspiration
Naomi

Wild Butterfly

Finding Your True North

Naomi Wayua Nyamai

Other books by Naomi Wayua Nyamai

Little Wild Butterfly

The butterfly said to the sun, "They can't stop talking about my transformation. I can only do it once in my lifetime. If only they knew, they can do it at any time and in countless ways."

— Dodinsky

Contents

Dedication

Thank you, God, my papa! I am loving this tango *(or is it a salsa dance)* we keep on doing every day together. Half the time I'm always trying to catch the rhythm of our beautiful dance in the ever changing seasons of life.

There are days we dance in the rain, sunshine, storms and even during the earthquakes and every time, you still hold me close to you. You manage to keep my focus on You despite the moments I am overcome with fear and anxiety of the unknown.

You are consistently present and remind me that I am not a prisoner of the environment we dance in. I have found unconditional love, true joy, safety, peace and belonging in your arms. I am no longer afraid because you are here with me, loving me unconditionally forever.

Dedication

Without the friendship, commitment and love of my family, my beloved and friends, I would have never shared a piece of myself in this book. Your love and encouragement has lifted me up and carried me through this broken world. You always remind me to be my own kind of beautiful. Thank you.

Then finally, to my two dogs, my rascals and companions—my boys *'Bruno'* and *'Troy'*. I'm certain people will always see you as just dogs, pets, or my savage guardians and wonder why I would dedicate my book to you too. To me, you have been true companions and partners in crime. You've taught me to be selfless and free spirited. My home will always be your home.

Naomi

An Invitation

This book was born from the inspiration of helping others find their true north. It's inspired by the caterpillar's journey to becoming a butterfly—one of the most fascinating and toughest transformation miracles that I've ever had the privilege of witnessing.

To anyone who is still trying to find themselves in one way or another, I dedicate this book to you. Let it be a reminder that you are a butterfly, giant, beautiful, and God's masterpiece. You are fearfully and wonderfully made in His own image.

Being a caterpillar is equally as beautiful as being a butterfly. It's a necessary stage we all need to embrace and allow to pass. Rise up from your ashes and transform as many times as you need to in your quest to find your True North.

An Invitation

Your True North is where you are ideally meant to be. It can sometimes be planned, random, or in-between. Sometimes, we find ourselves in limbo not knowing whether we are off track or on track. Regardless of your bearing, it's vital that you check in with yourself at the earliest possible time before you find yourself too far away from your ultimate destination. Worst case scenario, if you are lost, you can always find your way and eventually get where you need to be. Remember, all expeditions are never the same and they take different durations. The beauty behind those journeys lies in the miles you celebrate, lessons learnt, scars healed, wings grown and even the transformation that comes with it.

I cannot promise that you will get there today or tomorrow. I won't tell you it'll be easy, but one step ahead is one step closer to becoming your true self—a Wild Butterfly. Allow your wings to grow and your body to build enough muscle power to break through your cocoon and elevate you to the next level. Gradually develop your physical and mental strength, then you can fly and locate your True North.

Like any expedition, we desire to have companions who will go with us the whole mile. The truth is, half the time you may have to fly some miles alone, but that's still okay. You will still get there, and as they say, a journey of a thousand miles starts with a single step. It's always up to you to initiate that first single step.

Come and dance with me as we chase the butterflies on a personal journey of becoming a Wild Butterfly.

Here we go!

Not As It Seems

"There is nothing in a caterpillar that tells you
it's going to be a butterfly."

— Richard Buckminster Fuller

As a child, adventure and curiosity were part of who I was. There I was, living, learning, running, climbing, digging, and loving unapologetically. I climbed trees to try to discover what was beyond the clouds. Other times, you would find me doing my own expeditions on the soil beneath my feet just to find out what lived under the stones and behind the anthills on my father's farm. Every day was an adventure for me. There was always something to discover.

Every time I come across a butterfly, it takes me back to when I was 9 years old. When I was a child, I always marveled at the majestic splendour of a butterfly. I loved how it commanded attention across the globe and how its process of development is one of the most captivating there is.

I used to rush to throw stones to kill the little *"ugly"* caterpillars I would come across until one day my father heard me complain that the butterflies had avoided our home. That's when he said to me, *"Caterpillars and butterflies are the same thing Naomi."*

I was overwhelmed with guilt and sadness because of what I had done. From that day on, I not only allowed caterpillars to flourish in our garden but also picked some important life lessons that I would like to share with you.

I'm not sure if my father remembers this conversation as vividly as I do, but that particular memory is tattooed in my heart. It reminds me every day that not everything is what it seems.

Butterflies are one of the most beautiful insects found across the globe in various sizes and colours. You've probably come across one in your lifetime. If you're like me, you've probably tried to remain still so a butterfly can rest on your hand.

To become a butterfly, a caterpillar goes through a spectacular transformation referred to as metamorphosis. During this process the caterpillar is then transformed into a beautiful butterfly then after its wings have expanded and dried, it flies off.

Truth is, you can't have butterflies without caterpillars. That's why patience is a key virtue that I would like to highlight in this journey. Without patience you will never be able to get to watch a caterpillar transform into a butterfly.

Give yourself time to grow through to become all that you can be. Even if your present doesn't reflect an ounce of the life you are working towards, don't give up.

You're changing. Every day. In little invisible ways. Not everything is as it seems.

Even you.

The Courage to Be Authentic

"We crush the caterpillars
then complain there are no butterflies."

— Unknown

Most people are not moved by how caterpillars look or live because their outer appearance is not very captivating or attractive. Like I've said before, there is nothing in a caterpillar that tells you it's going to be a butterfly.

That's why we should always look beyond the surface. Focus more on your inner self as you embrace the process of becoming. Don't despise the unattractiveness of today's season for tomorrow. Work on strengthening your inner self.

We often find ourselves crushing the caterpillars then complain there are no butterflies. We are usually our own enemies. Let us take care of our caterpillar moments so that they can be nurtured into butterfly moments.

Some of us focus on working more on the outside than the inside. We buy stylish expensive clothes, make up, cars and expensive things to cover up for our weak inner lives.

You owe it to yourself to be whole on the inside. Never be apologetic about taking care of yourself. The most courageous quest I can challenge you to take on is to remove your mask and step out of your private space. Doing so is being brave and authentic. Even though it comes with the risk of being rejected or despised, you actually open the door to love and nurture yourself beyond what others see.

Why am I talking about masks? Well, masks are very common. We wear them every day in our different interactions with others. We wear them to protect our vulnerability and to cover our nakedness from others. Truth is, we all yearn to be accepted and appreciated for who we are. It takes courage to allow others to see and interact with our real selves. But the risk is always worth it.

Many people define beauty differently depending on how you look, behave and other parameters. For some, a woman's physical appearance is more important than their inner person. For others, how a person looks physically does not matter.

So, what is *true* beauty? Can it last? It is unwise for any woman to spend a lot of time and money on beauty products to become glamourous without making an effort to work on her character. It's not the make-up that helps us become better partners or mothers. It's the character we possess.

I remember my mother repeatedly reminding my sisters and I when we were blossoming into young ladies that the beauty of a woman, and even what makes a man attractive, is their character and sense of direction. That we shouldn't rely solely on physical appearance or the assets they own. There's always a need to focus on what is substantial; that which will not fade at all.

Search within. Look beyond and discover where you're at in your metamorphosis. This will help you focus on what really matters in your life to avoid stagnating in a cycle you don't understand.

Each season of life regardless of how fragile, complicated, different, beautiful, ugly, or painful plays a significant part in your life. It enables you to find your True North as you navigate the various climates of life.

Be kind to yourself. Love yourself. Never give up. Your transformation is taking place every day, every minute and every second you exist. It's inevitable. How you decide to handle it is what makes you a real game changer.

The Fragility of Time

"Just like the butterfly,
I too will awaken in my own time."

— Deborah Chaskin

The first time I took a 10 second breather with my eyes closed whilst sleeping on my back was when I was 14 years old. I was lying on the grass on a hot summer day at Hendon Park. The day couldn't be any better. We had gone for a family picnic with my sisters and my parents. After we were all stuffed, I decided to lie on my back and stare at the clouds up in the sky. The sky was so blue and clear.

There and then, I had an *aha* moment. I would stop everything in my mind, hold my breath and focus on anything I wanted for 10 seconds with my eyes closed.

When I opened my eyes, the grass seemed greener. There were kids younger than me playing football on the other side of the park. I could hear the laughter of other children, people talking and birds chirping. The sun's warmth was splendid. It was perfect in every way.

The world seemed to have stopped. I wanted to freeze and capture that moment. I had my favourite people with me in a beautiful spot. Our tummies were full with the sumptuous meals Mum had made.

Time…

That's what I thought I had. I wanted time to stop. My Papa and Mum were not in a hurry to go to work. We were not rushing to go to school. We were all there—present, alive, happy and together. We took pictures to remember that day.

Today, that day in the park is just another beautiful memory in my family member's minds and hearts. When I look back at it, I wonder why time had to pass. I realize that I am not a time magician. I can't stop time. The clock is always ticking. We get to grow up and evolve every day.

The lifespan of a human and a butterfly are not worthy of comparison as, unfortunately, butterflies do not have very long lifespans. Some live for a few months. However, the Brimstone butterfly gets to live up to 13 months. Imagine what it would take to make the best out of such a brief lifespan.

Let's be intentional with how we spend our time. Time is our friend yet, it's not patient with us. Let the memories we create matter and be worth the time we have invested in others. Never take people for granted and treasure moments with your loved ones.

Time is fragile. It's a gift and a privilege we cannot afford to ignore or take for granted.

Change is Inevitable

"We delight in the beauty of the butterfly, but rarely admit the changes it has gone through."

— Maya Angelou

Just like the lifecycle of a butterfly, change is inevitable. It's always just a matter of time. It's something we can't avoid because it's part of our lives. Because we are aware that change cannot be avoided, the best thing is for us to learn how to deal with it in the most effective way.

Some changes are painful, others are devastating. The fact that you know it's inevitable should help you remember that what you do with it is what really matters. Regardless of your age, race or colour, embrace change and the new cycle in your life.

I'd like to remind you of a monster that showed up and shook the whole world. Do you remember the Covid 19 pandemic? We are still living with that monster amongst us. It has changed all of our lives in one way or another—personally, professionally and even psychologically.

Many lives have been lost and every day is a war of survival. We have had no option but to face it head on. Thankfully, with the development of vaccines, the rate of infection and deaths has reduced significantly.

For me, Covid was initially a statistic I heard on the international news. Then, after some time, it came closer home. The statistical figures changed into names I knew. Then it came to my family's doorstep and pushed itself inside the house. My fear became a reality, and my reality became my testimony of God's grace.

Both of my parents had contracted Covid around the same time. It was a nightmare that had come to life and had no idea how we would deal with it. They were admitted in hospital and also needed a lot of care at home when they were discharged.

I remember getting a whole month off work just to look after them. Some of my friends recommended I let them care for each other isolated as they recuperated. I chose the opposite. I stayed home with them to look after them the whole time, ensuring we made it for the check-ups, encouraged them and prayed with them.

This new season of our lives drew us close to God and to each other. I knew I was exposed, and I wasn't sure whether we would make it. I'm glad we are all alive and God gave us another opportunity to see each new day since. My parents' journey of their recuperation taught me to be selfless and that love was never a word. Love is an action that speaks what it's in the heart.

As a family, we meet frequently to create new memories together and cherish our time with each other. Truth is, there is nothing special we did to deserve this second chance in life because Covid has taken so many people without notice. It is by God's grace and the power of his love and for that I can never thank Him enough.

I am more grateful, happier and never in a hurry to go through my hours or seconds in a day. I always knew that a day had 24 hours which had 60 seconds that make a minute. Now, time is a special machine for me. I no longer waste my time and energy chasing worthless things. I am more deliberate in how I spend my time and most importantly, I involve God in all my dealings.

A Jewel Called Contentment

"I am enough even if
I am a butterfly or a caterpillar."

— Unknown

When I look back at my life, I now clearly see how those changes have changed my life in a significant way. This inspires me even more when I think about the butterfly. I am very fascinated by how something becomes beautiful and I take time to notice the changes it went through.

Look at the successful people around you. I am sure they have heroic stories about how they got there. Their struggles, sacrifices and failures were a part of something great that was not clearly visible as they went through it.

Good things take time! That's what Mum always says

and she always said it when smiling even in the tough times.

Now I know why. Those tough seasons give you an opportunity to be grateful and to live a purposeful life.

There is this jewel called contentment which helps clothe us with grace in our everyday lives. Don't allow yourself to get lost in your journey of dealing with change. Let it refine you to become a better version of yourself.

It's also important to ask yourself what you need to feed on to become stronger to make it through the metamorphosis stage.

A caterpillar changing its state is not an easy process. It requires a healthy diet and a safe place. It needs vitamins and nutrients to go through all its changes so as to have a healthy transformation.

That's why it is important to nourish yourself in your transformation journey. You can start by gifting yourself with a smile, enough sleep, spending time with your loved ones and making time for your hobbies.

All these things are free and they will make sure you're content and thriving on the inside. After all, we all know that what's inside always shows up on the outside in one way or another.

Kiss The Rain

"Just living isn't enough," said the butterfly.
"One must have sunshine, freedom and a little flower."

— Hans Christian Anderson

Kiss me. Kiss me in the sunlight and my face will be radiant and glow like the noonday sun. Kiss me in the rain then my heart will come alive. I honestly find a kiss in the rain breathtaking because the love you feel is like a whirlwind. You only feel the cold of the rain after your heart has stopped pounding.

Just in case you are yet to try it, you should put it in your bucket list before you turn 50. Wait a minute. Did I say 50 years? Well, I meant as old or as young as you feel.

For me, kissing the rain is my ultimate definition

of breaking my barriers and reaching out to embrace the fear of the unknown. Though a butterfly looks fragile and timid, I find them brave. They go to new places and land on new leaf stalks and petals. There are days they let the sunshine kiss them, then there is the rain that sends them hiding.

Patience has neither been my forte nor my strength. I am always chasing the sunset. If I was a tree, I would be terrified of losing my leaves knowing they would never return. But in my ideal world, change would never break me or evoke any fear in my mind or heart. It would encourage me to embrace it as a natural process of life.

Where is the rain? *Who* is your rain? Life is about embracing the rain as much as you embrace the sunshine. The rain is part of the weather and it will always come and go at unexpected times. Though the sun will always seem like it sits on the throne, the rain is a visitor who will eventually show up and that is why it's vital to always prepare for it. And when it comes, step out and kiss the rain as you smile.

Will you love the kiss? Maybe you will. Maybe you won't. However, having in mind that the rain is a passing moment helps you deal with it. Life will always offer you rain. Some may come in the form of drizzles or even heavy downpour. Whatever the case, you need to invest in your inner self. That's the only way you can overcome your fears and kiss the rain.

Here's to dancing, kissing the rain and believing that triumph is on the other side of tribulation. You can be whoever you want to be, as unique as that may be. The storms that come with the rain don't define who you are.

The Courage to Begin Again

"Life without pain is a life spent in a cocoon. You have to break the cocoon to experience your beauty."

— Shubhi

Every day, people are in their own spaces trying to lift up their heads and hearts above the storms of life. We are all trying to courageously balance the things on our plates of life.

It's important to take care of your mental and physical self. Doing so helps you hold on to your identity and truth such that you are not defined by the inner climatic changes in your life. Rather, the inner climatic conditions you are exposed to help you to reinvent yourself as many times as you need to be the best version of yourself.

I remember several instances where I was trying to

catch my breath because I had moments of anxiety, panic, sadness and grief. Half the time, nothing made sense. I guess I have felt like a broken jar more times than I've felt like a flower vase. But every time, courage and the grace of God always came to fill me up. My broken jar or flower vase always was full. This helped me to always begin again, and again. I guess that who we are—human. Fragile, and beautiful at the same time.

I hadn't realized how fragile I was until my tears and heartbreak overwhelmed me. It took me several days to take a step back, breathe and start working on getting back on my feet. Otherwise, I was heading into a bottomless pit of depression, one that would turn me into a woman I knew nothing about.

Every single day after that was a deliberate effort to live well and find peace. It's true what they say. Peace is expensive. You have to work really hard to get there.

The nights and days become longer in a beautiful way and even though I am still on my journey, I can confidently say that I am honestly happy, at peace and content. I no longer get anxiety attacks or sacrifice my joy and peace of mind to please the people in my life.

I guess for me, the greatest lesson I learnt from a butterfly is that just living isn't enough. There's so much more to life. That's how I decided I wanted to live my life. I continually choose to pursue happiness each single day.

I can recall how I have made a great effort finding myself and trying to discover what my purpose for existence is. In the process, I have learned to embrace both the good and tough times keeping in mind that not all seasons or situations are permanent.

Set yourself free. Step out of your comfort zone. Make the most of your opportunities and allow yourself to feel these moments. It will make you stronger, bolder and more confident.

You are always free to reinvent yourself as many times as possible so that you give yourself an opportunity to become the butterfly that you are.

Nurture Yourself

"A season of loneliness and isolation is when the caterpillar gets its wings. Remember that next time you feel alone."

— Mandy Hale

Can you remember what you wanted to be when you grew up or what were your fears? Well, I do. I wanted to be an astronaut. I wanted to discover what used to lie behind the stars that light the evening sky.

I also wanted to be an explorer who could discover the world barefoot. Yes, barefoot. As a child, I would race with the wind without any shoes on. I loved how the earth felt beneath my feet. But sometimes, those adventures gave me blisters. With time, I learnt to live without forgetting to care for and protect myself and those around me.

Nothing gave me more pleasure than the feeling of freedom, peace and happiness. When I was a child, I used to see the world as an endless football pitch which I could always play on whenever I wanted. I could feel and hear the sound of freedom from my heart.

I have a personal rule: *love yourself.* Every part of you. Your core essence, your mind, your body and your soul. Pursue what makes you happy and you will never feel like you are trying to survive through your day. Rather, work on gliding through the day. You need to prioritize and ensure there are things you can do just for you.

Did you know that a butterfly's diet is a strictly liquid diet consisting of nectar and sweet tree sap?

Just like a butterflies, it's important to pursue the things that make you happy. A healthy body is a healthy person. You need to take care of your physical wellbeing so that you don't expose yourself to disease as a result of malnutrition.

Take care of your mind. What you choose to consume affects what you give out. Garbage in, garbage out. Be intentional about what you store in your mind and heart each day.

Make it a priority to care for both your physical and mental well-being. It's not an easy task especially if you are caring for others, but it's worth it.

Personal care and love needs to be deliberate. Take time to nurture yourself. A full day consists of 24 hours. I am sure you can allocate some time for yourself daily. Set the rhythm and you will be surprised how time coupled with personal care improves both your physical and mental health.

In most of our self-care journeys, we find ourselves experiencing moments of loneliness and isolation. If we are not careful, we can get caught up in a web of setbacks and depression. I have learned that being alone at times is not a bad thing. It has taught me to appreciate my journey. Showing up for myself is key.

Don't get me wrong, friends, partners and family are important, however, for whatever strange reason, should they fail to show up on time or never show up in the tough or best moments in your life, please don't beat yourself up. It's okay. At least show up for yourself.

Did you know that in a cocoon, a caterpillar is usually alone and isolated? It's during this season of loneliness and isolation that a caterpillar gets its wings. You might be all by your lonesome right now, but in a little while, if you do the time, you'll be ready to fly.

An Elevated Life

"Soar up high with the beauty
and grace of a butterfly."

— Unknown

Did you know that caterpillars are born to creep and crawl but are reborn to fly? They shed off their old life and emerge from their chrysalis to become the butterflies they are destined to be. Butterflies experience the world from a new and elevated vantage point.

In the same way, when believers are born again to the newness of life in Christ, they see things from God's perspective. According to Romans 12:2, we are reminded to not copy the behaviour and customs of this world, but to let God transform us into new people by changing the way we think. This is how we will learn to know God's good, pleasing and perfect will for us.

Have you had a chance to have a look at dead and decaying matter? Is it not a terrible sight? For a caterpillar, that is its food in addition to plant leaves. Degenerate souls feed on the deadly toxins of a life devoted to sin. But born-again believers attach themselves to Jesus Christ, the true source of life.

We are reminded about God's essence and helping us bear fruit.

> "I am the vine; you are the branches. If you remain in me and I in you, you will bear much fruit; apart from me you can do nothing."
>
> — John 15:5

Butterflies drink sweet nectar from flowering plants. Once believers taste and see that the Lord is good *(Psalm 34:8)*, they begin to feed on God's word and are nourished by it *(1 Peter 2:1–3)*. In Christ, they receive a new, eternal nature. They become spiritually alive and free as God intended them to be.

> "Since you have heard about Jesus and have learned the truth that comes from him, throw off your old sinful nature and your former way of life, which is corrupted by lust and deception.

> Instead, let the Spirit renew your thoughts and attitudes. Put on your new nature, created to be like God—truly righteous and holy."
>
> — Ephesians 4:21–24

A transformation like that of a caterpillar to a butterfly lifts new believers up and out of the darkened path of the world into freedom and wholeness of kingdom life.

> "But you are a chosen people, a royal priesthood, a holy nation, God's special possession, that you may declare the praises of him who called you out of darkness into his wonderful light."
>
> — 1 Peter 2:9

This is *true* transformation. This is the *ultimate* transformation that will set the pace for everything else in your life. Align your course with God's, our True North, and you are sure to be on the right path no matter every wind of change or trouble.

The Butterfly Effect

"The fluttering of a butterfly's wings can affect climate changes on the other side of the planet."

— Paul Ehrlich

Have you ever thought about how magnificent a little thing can be? Having the ability to make a difference is important. Knowing that you have the potential to be part of a bigger plan or make a difference is an even greater power. No impact or contribution is ever too small. Every little thing counts and any contribution, regardless of how small, matters.

Martin Luther King is no stranger to us. His name is mentioned in conversations of greatness. He managed to change the world by stirring the air with his own wings and set in motion changes that would upend some of the foundations of the Roman Catholic church. He took a small step in his local environment and this contribution spurred massive changes that shook the world.

Someone else that gives me great inspiration is Nehemiah from the Bible. He isn't highly regarded by many but I find him very inspiring and a change-maker. Unlike some of the other heroes we all know about in the Bible, Nehemiah was not a prophet, king, or even a priest. He wasn't from the lineage of Christ or one of the twelve disciples.

Can you imagine that not one miracle took place in his lifetime? He had heard about God's promises despite growing in a culture that questioned God's justice, love and sovereignty to His people. Yet, he clung to the beliefs and practices that he learnt as a child.

One day as I studied book of Nehemiah, I was moved by Nehemiah's heart. When we think about the walls of Jerusalem, his name comes to mind. Without his efforts to rebuild the wall, most Israelites would not have returned home.

This was not just a physical wall. It was a safe haven and their fortress. The Jews had returned home after 70 years in exile and everything was in ruins. Nehemiah rebuilt the wall in 52 days. It's a huge task that reminds me about the butterfly effect that states that a small action sparks a gigantic change.

Sometimes, we run away from making an impact by being selective in the projects we pursue. It's human nature to always pick the easy, convenient, and cheapest path. After all, why should we make something our sole responsibility when there are other people who have the muscle to step in and help?

Be faithful in the little things and desire to make a difference regardless of how large or small things may be. It's not about the size but the motive behind it.

Did you know that less than five hundred years after Nehemiah completed the wall with his team, Jesus Christ made his way to Jerusalem on a donkey and saw the beautiful, giant and majestic walls?

Without the walls, there would be no city.

No city, no people.

And no people means who would have the Messiah come to see?

Let us not sit back and patiently wait for the *'important people'* to be the only ones that trigger waves of impact and change in our communities and eventually the world.

Minor Adjustments

"Butterflies are self-propelled flowers,"

— Robert A. Heinlein

For some strange reason, I am drawn to my reflection and I often search within my heart for the status of my transformation from a butterfly to a caterpillar. I usually use my mirror moments as a moment of reflection and affirmation.

I'd love for you to try it. Take a pause from what you're doing right now and take a look at yourself in the mirror. Ask yourself:

What can I do?
Who is the person staring back at me? Do I recognize them?
Where is my heart?
What is my vision?

Am I in love with the person staring back at me?

What do I have to bring to the table?

Do I just see a mere stranger staring back at me?

I didn't mean to get heavy and deep on you but these mirror moments are very powerful. Do them as often as you can and they will help you course correct on your journey of transformation.

You need to give yourself a chance to elevate your potential. We are often our biggest enemies when we devalue our contribution in many ways. You lose nothing when you share your thoughts and ideas.

There is no idea or change that is too small. Birth the littles changes and give them a chance to evolve as they make a difference in the lives of people.

Sometimes, when you wait for other people to affirm your contribution, it may work against you. Sometimes others will affirm you while others will not but it does not devalue your contribution. Make your contribution and invest in yourself. You need to be your biggest cheerleader and affirmer.

Your ability to appreciate yourself and care for yourself helps you build a strong backbone on which you can make the first flutter of your wings.

Every flight begins with a flutter. Yes, you heard me right. All it takes is a flutter to fly to endless places and change the world to a better place.

Did you know that a little flutter of your wings can make a significant change? Flutter your wings with courage.

When you grow tired and weary, take some time off and rest and recharge. Then flutter your wings once more. Just don't flutter them too much and lose your breath while at it.

Always know your lane and where you are heading then flutter strategically towards your True North.

Time and Seasons

"The butterfly counts not months but moments,
and has time enough."

— Rabindranath Tagore

I remember visiting Trafalgar Square for the first time in my life when I was twelve years old. Sitting on the lion statues next to the water fountain and feeding pigeons with so much excitement in the warm sun is a potent memory I carry.

"Papa, Mummy, look!" I would shout feeding the pigeons. *"They are not biting my hand."* I wasn't afraid that they would peck me because my sister's courage had also sparked courage in me.

It was a hot summer day, and I was excited that we

were outdoors, rather than at home watching TV. I wanted time to stand still and the moment to last forever. It was one of the most beautiful places my parents had taken me and my two sisters during that particular summer.

Trafalgar Square is one of the most visited places in London. It's a public square in the city of Westminster, central London that was established in the 19th century. The Square's name commemorates the Battle of Trafalgar, the British naval victory in the Napoleonic wars over France and Spain.

The square is full of many tourists and street musicians who play live performances. In the same space, there was a water fountain, the biggest I had ever seen and I remember trying to climb from the sides to check if there were any fish. There were none, but I saw many shiny coins spread inside the water fountain.

I could hear people making wishes verbally, while others just murmured. Some believed that wishes could come true if you threw a coin and made a wish at the wishing fountain. It's a common European folklore that you may have heard about. I threw my coin into the fountain and made my wish. I would tell you what my wish was but I'm awfully shy.

Every summer, I would always desire to go there. That's the thing about Trafalgar Square. It steals you away into a new whole world. You forget about everything that exists outside of it.

When you look at a butterfly and its world, it's very different from our world. It's less complicated and full of beauty.

Some people believe that if one makes a wish by throwing a coin into a wishing well, from each wish a butterfly is born. It's a little too whimsical for my liking but luckily, I have a vivid imagination.

Water is essential to a butterfly for its survival. It drinks it and also uses it to cool down from the hot temperatures. Just as a butterfly visits a water fountain to replenish itself, where do you find yourself heading to recharge? Where is your foundation? Where do you go to reenergize, heal, find your sanity or quench your thirst?

The world will always offer us many wishing wells or water fountains. Some may look grander than Trafalgar Square. But the real question is, where is your fountain? For me, my wishing well is the Bible that has the word of God where I can continuously plug in to grow my faith and recharge to face the different seasons in my life.

You probably have a favourite place you run to when your current space overwhelms you. That place is a place of beauty and peace. Running is always easy. However, making your current space beautiful and memorable is usually the hardest thing ever.

Do you evoke storms or calm breezes to the people you meet? Some of us are like hurricanes. We have no respect for the people we meet. We just bring destruction and destroy anybody who is on our way.

This is a rare courage—choosing to be the beauty or the essence of peace in the places you reside and the people you interact with.

What We're Up Against

"As with the butterfly, adversity is necessary
to build character in people."

— Joseph B. Wirthlin

The seasons remind me of the metamorphosis process of a butterfly. Spring, summer, fall, and winter are the four seasons. Each has its own light, temperature, and weather patterns that take place yearly.

Each season, though different, depicts beauty. There is beauty in embracing the seasons we experience in life, not taking them for granted and making the best out of each one.

There's a friend, or should I call her an enemy, who is my daily companion that means a million and one things to others. My friend's name is time. We always feel we have enough of her and there are days we feel she is scarce.

The truth is, time will never wait for us. It's like a continuous never ending pendulum that keeps moving at all times. What matters is what you do about it.

Did you know that a butterfly only lives for a few weeks and within that time, it manages to accomplish its life mission? The average lifespan of a butterfly runs between 3 to 4 weeks with the entire cycle lasting between two to eight months.

However, there is a species of a butterfly that lives for approximately 24 hours while some migratory butterflies, like the North American Monarch, can survive for nearly eight months.

Time is what we are up against. How long will it take you evolve from your egg, then become a caterpillar and eventually become a butterfly before your time is up? Will you wait to be 50 years or 80 years to start desiring a significant transition of your life?

There is no time. The time is now. The point when you realize that you need to embrace your metamorphosis is the only point that you can start evolving. Otherwise, you will remain in your cocoon while your time continues to run out.

If a butterfly's existence spans around 7 to 8 weeks

and human life expectancy is up to 80 years old, what does that mean to you? You have a longer opportunity to become the wild butterfly you need to become. Still, we often stagnate and cannot break free from the cycle of oppression.

You need to ask yourself whether you are a prisoner of life and if so, what are the things or people who keep pulling you back to the place of stagnation.

Ask yourself if you are your own worst enemy. Assess your life for the vices that I have prevented you from making the best of your time here on earth.

This Scripture bring it out well.

> "There is a time for everything, and a season for every activity under the heavens: a time to be born and a time to die, a time to plant and a time to uproot, a time to kill and a time to heal, a time to tear down and a time to build, a time to weep and a time to laugh, a time to mourn and a time to dance, a time to scatter stones and a time to gather them, a time to embrace and a time to refrain from embracing, a time to search and a time to give up, a time to keep and a time to throw away, a time to tear and a time to mend, a time to be silent and a time to speak, a time to love and a time to hate, a time for war and a time for peace."
>
> — Ecclesiastes 3:1-8

The realization that seasons come and go is part of our humanity. What you do in the various seasons of your life is very important. When it's a season of planting, you should be planting so that when the season of harvesting comes you have something to gather from the soil to avoid starving or borrowing from others as a result of your laziness.

Seasons and time are related. You cannot separate the two. You need to learn how to live and not just exist.

Now that I reminded you about the essence of time, what does that mean for you? What will you pivot your strengths and willpower towards? Whatever it is, commit to act as your choice will impact the quality of life you would like to live.

To live has always been a grand adventure for me. Living without the appreciation of life itself scares me out of my wits. I have always been afraid to wake up and realize that there is no time and my bucket list is still not even half done.

You may not always be able to accomplish all that you have set out to do, but at least you can challenge yourself to do something instead of nothing.

Because of this, I am kind to myself. I will run my race just like a butterfly and know it will be worthwhile to go through my cycle regardless of how long it takes. I have the courage to go through my metamorphosis like a real butterfly.

Welcome Home

"We are all butterflies.
Earth is our chrysalis."

— LeeAnn Taylor

Home is a special place that we hold dear. It's a place that keeps you safe. It's free from discrimination and offers you refuge. Butterflies know their homes. They know the places they can live and coexist with other creatures within a conducive environment fit for their survival.

I was fascinated to learn that butterflies are found everywhere on earth except Antarctica because of its extreme climate incapable of sustaining the life of a butterfly.

The North American Monarch butterfly intrigues me. Its annual migration is epic, unique and an amazing phenomenon.

Did you know that it is the only butterfly that makes a two way migration journey like birds?

Unlike other species of butterflies that overwinter as larvae, pupae, or even as adults, Monarchs cannot survive the cold weather associated with winters. Thus, they use environmental cues to make their journey strategically.

They combine thermals, the position of the sun, the earth's magnetic pull and air currents to help them make their journey which is usually a long distance. Some travel up to 3,000 miles to reach their destination.

Monarchs in Eastern North America have a second home in the Sierra Madre Mountains of Mexico. Monarchs in Western North America overwinter in California.

Did you know that they can travel between 50-100 miles a day? That means it can take up to two months to complete their journey. The farthest ranging Monarch butterfly recorded traveled 265 miles in one day.

Not only do they travel for a long distance, they travel in swarms. A cluster can consist of tens and thousands on a tree. This offers them protection, guidance and a sense of belonging. It is usually very difficult for a butterfly to separate itself from the group. This massive movement of butterflies has been called one of the most spectacular natural phenomena in the world. One thing that struck me is that every generation born does not get lost. It's like they always know they are part of something great—a journey or mission they must complete.

You have to understand the critical difference between the Magnetic North and True North. When you don't understand the difference, you will think you are going in the right direction then you end up missing your ultimate destination. True North will always lead you directly to the North Pole.

In 2002, the Magnetic North was 590 miles away from the True North, but that distance also changes from time to time based upon the strength of the pull of the earth's magnetic core.

In relation to this, look at the Spirit of God as your guide and our destination is your True North. We often wander across life towards a particular destination like the legendary Monarch butterflies.

Some people may refer to that destination as our ultimate purpose of existence while others perceive it as utopia, their paradise. We need to allow ourselves to be led by God so that we don't stray from the correct course of our journeys in our lives.

There is a Magnetic North that will always lead us away from the right path. As humans, we have predominant patterns similar to the magnetic pull that deceives us that we are walking in the right direction yet we are on the wrong path. This compass tells us we are going North yet we are 590 miles off and don't know it.

Following your Magnetic North will discourage you on your journey because it won't take you where you thought it would so you will never seem to arrive.

When you are travelling, it's always reassuring when you know your destination and are sure about how to get there. For accurate navigation, finding the True North is vital and helps us follow the right path. When our navigational bearing is tampered with, it evokes a feeling of anxiety and to some extent fear.

These Scriptures remind us about our True Magnetic compass.

> "When the Spirit of truth comes, he will guide you into all the truth, for he will not speak on his own authority, but whatever he hears he will speak, and he will declare to you the things that are to come. He will glorify me, for he will take what is mine and declare it to you. All that the Father has is mine; therefore I said that he will take what is mine and declare it to you."
> — John 16:13-15

> "For who knows a person's thoughts except the spirit of that person, which is in him? So also no one comprehends the thoughts

> of God except the Spirit of God. Now we have received not the spirit of the world, but the Spirit who is from God, that we might understand the things freely given us by God."
>
> — 1 Corinthians 2:11–12

We need to trust in God to be the one that leads us and listen to the Holy Spirit's guidance so that we are able to migrate just like the Monarch butterflies with a purpose and make it to our ultimate destination. The infallible and trustworthy guide in our lives is the Spirit of God.

Make Peace with Time

"We are like butterflies who flutter for a day
and think it is forever."

— Carl Sagan

When I was a little girl, I loved running and chasing the wind on my father's farm and loved to hear the sound of his tractor mowing our land. How I loved running across every corner and discovering the treasures that were in the farm.

Our farm was a place I used to go almost every time school used to close. My heart and spirit felt free there. Maybe it was the innocence of my childhood that took me to that place.

Then something happened to me. I grew up and realized something called time. My constant reminder was how I can't control it and every day, I lose a day of my existence.

I remember a few years back when I was starting off in my career and becoming a woman. Things were tough. I would sometimes rush into empty boardrooms or my car to seek refuge or to take a breather. Sometimes, I would struggle to fit in. Other times, my bosses or work was demanding. Then there was my love life which was also another toxic ingredient adding to my anxiety and stress.

My dreams and aspirations sometimes felt far off and hard to reach. I spent most of my years trying to catch up with my peers and this led to physical and emotional fatigue. The day I realized everyone has their own race to run, I began to run my own. I was finally able to catch my breath. I was now able to breathe and be patient to myself.

Breathe and be patient! That is one of the most important lessons I have learnt from a butterfly. Butterflies remind us that all good things take time. It takes a butterfly time to evolve from one stage of life to another until it eventually becomes a butterfly. Simply be kind and patient as you change and evolve into the best version of yourself.

The more I learnt to give myself a chance to move at my pace in both my professional and personal life, my inner joy, peace and physical health changed for the better. With time, I fell deeper in love with myself and discovered how important I was to God and the people around me. I no longer desired to entertain fake relationships that were unhealthy or to waste my time chasing non valuable things.

Breathing and patience will help you find the rhythm of how to live meaningfully so you are able to make and achieve sustainable goals in your life. Time is neither your friend nor enemy so stop fighting it. Rather, invest your time and energy into making the best out of it.

Create time to take yourself out for a date or participate in an activity you love. You are here today. Let your now cushion your tomorrow. Be deliberate in spending time with your loved ones.

Try smiling or laughing more often. Yes! Smile. It will light up your soul and improve both your emotional and physical being. Smiling can help you manage stress and anxiety by releasing endorphins—the chemicals that make you happier.

It's not always the first to arrive that are happiest. After all, the goal is to arrive at your destination. Move forward and grow at your own pace. Don't let all the other 'noises' distract you. You'll get there in your own time and, hopefully, happier.

I Am A Wild Butterfly

"I embrace emerging experience. I participate in discovery.
I am a butterfly. I am not a butterfly collector.
I want the experience of the butterfly."

— William Stafford

One day, you will wake up and live with contentment where loving you and having your peace of mind is okay. One day, you will no longer rush around like a headless chicken desperate to seek affirmation, pursue broken dreams or nurture toxic relationships. When this moment comes, embrace it. Allow yourself to feel everything—the emotions, the winds, the hurricanes, and the warmth of the sunlight.

If you are not here yet, seek to get here. Then you will stop existing and start living a more holistic and full life. There is a delicate balance that you need to selfishly guard as you seek to become the person you have always wanted to be. It is very crucial to take care of yourself in this season to ensure you equip yourself with the right things.

Taking care of both your physical and mental wellbeing should be your priority. Cherish and spoil yourself. Make it a priority to date yourself and treat yourself with care. After all, your body is the only place you have to live in.

Time has been one of my greatest gifts. It's been a teacher and healer in my journey. It's funny how I look back and see how far I have come and all the moments I took things for granted. These days, I am taking my time to enjoy every aspect of it. I have intentionally become cautious of my minutes, hours, days, months and years.

A wild butterfly is characterized by being in a stage of your life where you have learnt to accept yourself. One where you can actually look at yourself in the mirror and tell yourself that it's okay to love and be kind to yourself. A place where you will not allow your self worth be measured by other people's standards or opinions.

My caterpillar golden rules that have kept me going are:

- **Contentment** in every season you are in

- **Affirm:** Remind yourself of the limitless possibilities you can attain
- **Try:** Never give up, always chose to get up when you fall
- **Embrace** your season
- **Remember** your journey and the great plans you've set out to achieve
- **Pray** and ask God to help you find your purpose on this planet
- **Influence:** Step in a space and command respect
- **Love** yourself
- **Learn** to laugh and find joy
- **Act:** Put your dreams into action so that they can be a reality
- **Rise** up from the status quo

Being a wild butterfly means that you have embraced the metamorphosis process fully and have accepted to pay the cost. It's a very expensive venture when you think about it.

2 Corinthians 5:17 reminds us that those who belong to Christ have become a new creation, the old life is no more and they can now begin a new life. God changes the caterpillar into a butterfly.

I dare you to be a wild butterfly, untamed and free!

Honouring the Metamorphosis Process

"Butterflies are nature's tragic heroes. They live most of their lives being completely ordinary. And then, one day, the unexpected happens. They burst from their cocoons on their own in a blaze of colors and become utterly extraordinary. It is the shortest phase of their lives, but it holds the greatest importance."

— Kelseyleigh Reber

That second in the minute of that day when you transform is what I like to call your sparkle moment. It's like the moment a caterpillar bursts from its cocoon on its own in a blaze of colours to become an utterly extraordinary butterfly. This moment is worth celebrating and calling out. I think it is a moment of bravery. An epic hero moment.

How long do you have to live? Are you privy to the day your life here on earth will end? The longevity of life remains a key mystery to us. The best that we can do is make each moment we are alive count and make the best of every day. Don't take your life for granted because it's a gift from God and not a right that you deserve.

Because butterflies undergo metamorphosis, throughout the world they are symbols of transformation, change, rebirth, and even resurrection. Honour your own metamorphosis and that of others. This takes deliberate effort. It means that you're intentional to appreciate everyone's journey and yours too.

Embracing your transformation process from a caterpillar to a butterfly to help you build muscle and refine your character. Most people expect the metamorphosis process to break you. Truth is, it can. The flip side is also true when they say what doesn't break you makes you stronger. That's why it is paramount that you make it a habit of making the best of the tough times.

A chrysalis is what a caterpillar forms when it begins its metamorphosis. This is characterized by a solitude retreat for a period of time. They are alone with no outer disturbance to enable them to complete their transformation. Solitude usually gives us some space to connect and work on our inner selves in our metamorphosis. This is a conscious choice we have to make unlike the butterfly as part of our beautiful and epic transformation journey.

Take risks. It's a very important part of this process. If you never gather courage to take risks, you will never know how beautiful you can become. Stretch yourself and know that risk takers always go far. It takes courage to be a risk taker. I was always shy about being one myself. Then one day, I jumped my metaphorical hill.

Risks do not guarantee you success in all your battles. You will definitely win some and also lose some. And that's okay. Every failure is an opportunity to learn.

Something else you need to look out for is resistance. We adorn ourselves with it as our Sunday best attire or a war armour. Sometimes, it turns out to be the ultimate weapon of destruction to ourselves and also to others. You cannot resist your metamorphosis journey. We all have to evolve and grow regardless of where we live in the world. It is always reassuring when we know the outcomes of events. But we are often afraid when we are not in control.

The aspect of not knowing how something might play

out may scare some of us while sparking excitement and a sense of adventure in others. When you know how you're likely to respond, it will help you adjust on your metamorphosis journey.

Even When It Hurts

"What if the change you are avoiding
is the one that gives you wings?"

— Unknown

When I was young, my parents used to make me and my siblings to do various chores. Little did I know that some of those things that we were required to do helped shape us into more responsible adults.

Chores aren't fun. They're tedious but necessary to ensure the smooth running of any home. Any child would rather be outside, playing with friends, or watching TV than doing a chore. Chores are often the hard good training we go through when young in preparation for life.

Allow me to share with you a famous story that has

become one of my favourites in recent years. It's a story about a man, a butterfly, nature, good intentions, pity and selflessness that led to a disaster. Just like any other story, it has a message that I think is worth considering.

> A man found a cocoon of a butterfly. One day a small opening appeared. He sat and watched the butterfly for several hours as it struggled to squeeze its body through the tiny hole. Then it stopped, as if it couldn't go further. So the man decided to help the butterfly. He took a pair of scissors and snipped off the remaining bits of cocoon. The butterfly emerged easily but it had a swollen body and shriveled wings.
>
> The man continued to watch it, expecting that any minute the wings would enlarge and expand enough to support the body, Neither happened! In fact the butterfly spent the rest of its life crawling around. It was never able to fly. What the man in his kindness and haste did not understand: The restricting cocoon and the struggle required by the butterfly to get through the opening was a way of forcing the fluid from the body into the wings so that it would be ready for flight once that was achieved.
>
> Sometimes struggles are exactly what we need in our lives. Going through life with no obstacles would cripple us. We will not be as strong as we could have been and we would never fly.
>
> — Author Unknown

The struggles we go through just like the butterfly prepare us for flight. They shape our character, sharpen our wit, mould our courage and strengthen our muscles. We become crippled when we are supported too much that we become dependent on other people and unable to function alone.

The Power of Influence

"A rare butterfly is born from the society that is chaotic.
It was never going to exist any other way."

— J.L. Haynes

As long as people have wondered about the world, they have been intrigued by the mysteries of human nature. As human beings, we desire to connect and be understood. The magic behind this is bringing to life what we feel and think in such a way that we can be understood. We communicate both verbally and non-verbally with people we engage with.

Did you know that butterflies communicate mostly through chemical signals. Males produce pheromones to attract females. A few species communicate with sound. For example, the male Cracker Butterfly can produce noises with its wings.

Communication with others allows us to express ourselves better and also learn from others. It's an essential skill that we cannot ignore in our transformation journey. There is value in sharing from your end but you also need to appreciate feedback as much as your output.

We often learn how to communicate and lead from an early age as our families are the basic schools of orientation but communication is a skill we need to sharpen over the years.

To achieve your intended results when communicating, you first need to establish a clear purpose. What do you want your audience to know as a result of your message? What do you want them to do? You will usually find what you have one of the general purposes: to inform, persuade and instruct.

A communicator needs to find out how best to package and deliver their message effectively to their desired target group.They also need to ensure that the audience will always seek to make sense out of the message presented to them.

Poor communication can greatly affect a person's leadership ability. Human communication is very essential in life since it enables us to achieve individual and group goals much more effectively. There are many leaders who have not been effective as agents of change because of poor mastery of their communication skills.

Communication is a powerful tool. When we are unable to effectively transmit our message and not able to comprehend the feedback, then we will be unable to be as effective in our daily executions.

Just like a butterfly always finds a way to communicate and be understood, we need to master this vital aspect of communication.

I would like to urge you to see yourself as part of a great transformation agenda. Your purpose is extraordinary. I call upon you to be a person who is an ambassador or a leader of influence.

Be the kind of leader who communicates effectively so you can propel the winds of change and positive transformation regardless of your age, gender, religion or even tribe.

I See You

"Butterflies can't see their wings. They can't see
how truly beautiful they are, but everyone else can.
People are like that as well."

— Unknown

It's strange how you can sometimes not recognize your beauty yet the people around you can. We need to be conscious that our lives, however private, have an ability to influence other people. For instance, butterflies are unaware that we have been studying and learning so much from them for such a long time. Through their epic transformation journey, we can be inspired to transform to become better.

Are you willing to allow your transformation journey to change lives by inspiring others or will you hide it from those around you?

How do you show up every day, in your place of work and even in social contexts? What fruits do you bear or share with others?

They say that actions speak louder than words so it is important for us to be conscious of our actions regardless of where we are or who we are with. There is always someone watching, learning, and unlearning our behaviour.

Butterfly Gardens

"Don't waste your time chasing butterflies.
Mend your garden, and the butterflies will come."

— Mario Quintana

When you are mentally healthy, you will find it easier to interact with people and understand yourself better. True transformation needs to be a personal decision.

Others can inspire or challenge you, but if you don't decide to kick start your metamorphosis, you may never fully evolve to the next best version of yourself.

Let's make a garden

It has been said that something as small as the flutter

of a butterfly's wing can ultimately cause a typhoon halfway around the world. I invite you to be part of something great by becoming a backyard butterfly conservationist.

Even as you reflect on your metamorphosis journey, I hope you are able to celebrate your caterpillar moments and enjoy the ride as you evolve into your own beautiful version of a butterfly.

You matter. Every single part of you. Your process of growth is beautiful. It doesn't matter what angle anyone looks at it from. It's still your unique journey that people may choose to not be part of or show up when you need them the most.

Show up for yourself. You need to start showing up for yourself instead of always looking at the door hoping a superhero would walk in and save you. Have you ever stopped to wonder that a superhero not showing up is the best case scenario?

One of the most rewarding ways to help butterflies is to create a butterfly habitat in your own garden. This small exercise may look small but you are playing a bigger role in butterfly conservation.

You can choose to plant trees and flowers to host the butterflies, feed them or make a home for them at your residence. Butterflies use their sense of smell to locate nectar in plants instead of using their sight.

How can you become a backyard butterfly conservationist? It's a simple exercise that you cannot afford to miss out on. Below are some of the things you need to prepare to make your garden a success.

- Water and hydration
- Shelter
- The sun
- No pesticides or toxins
- Peace and quiet

Let's go through each one of them, shall we?

Hydrate and Recharge

"Live life like a butterfly.
Take a rest. But never forget how to fly."

— Unknown

Where do you draw inspiration from and how do you recharge? This is worth considering.

Nectar, tree sap and dew provide butterflies with water. You can create a puddling station for butterflies by getting a shallow dish, fill with gravel or sand and put it in your garden sheltered from naked sun and wind.

As you build your butterfly garden, ensure you put some water and sprinkle some salt to dampen it but do not flood the dish. The puddle will attract butterflies during the hot weather to cool off their bodies.

The little salt you have sprinkled is a delicacy for them. It's actually the reason why butterflies like to rest on our sweaty hands and palms but don't let this fact ruin that magical moment.

To fully go through a healthy metamorphosis process, one needs to intentionally take in the right nutrients both physically and mentally.

What you feed your body, mind and soul goes a long way to promote a healthy transition or growth. Invest in your mental wellness, eat good healthy meals, rest and spend time with good friends. This will help you cultivate a healthy lifestyle, not a toxic one.

Create A Shelter

We all need a safe place to go to when life gets hard. A place of refuge to protect us from the elements and outside forces. Butterfies are very similar to us in this regard.

Where do you find refuge?

Ensure there are plenty of trees and reasonable shrubs that will provide some shade and food for the butterflies. This place needs to be safe from predators and strong winds.

This means you need to plant flowers in your garden area and clear out any plastic or metal waste. Butterflies usually seek shelter to feed, relax, hydrate and also to mate, therefore the shelter needs to facilitate their comfort.

Where do you feel safe? Where is your refuge? Psalm 46 says that God is our refuge and strength, a very present help in trouble. The reality is that there will be difficult times, but God promises to be our refuge.

Where you seek refuge is important because it informs how well you deal with things especially on the difficult days when things don't make sense. I usually find this verse very comforting because it reminds me that I always have God with me any time, any day to watch over me.

Cultivate a relationship with your creator so that He continuously walks with you on your growth journey. The people you spend time with matter. Negative people with ill motives will always give negative energy. Be very intentional about your personal space. Protect your physical and mental haven. Peace should be a priority to you. Guard it without apology.

A Little Bit of Sunlight

When I was 20 years old exploring books at my university while pursuing my first degree, I came across a strange book. I can't seem to recall the author, but I remember a sentence that caught my eye on the back cover. It was in bold. *'Keep me where the light is!'*

The light that the sun depicted in the book gave hope and light so much that every time the sun visited, the darkness quickly tiptoed away.

How magnificent is the sun!

To create a backyard butterfly garden, select an area of your garden that will get at least 5-6 hours of sunlight daily. Butterflies delight sun basking despite being cold-blooded. Apart from sun basking on leaves and large rocks, butterflies need to enjoy the sun but not get burned by it.

As you seek to build your inner butterfly garden, what are the things that brighten up your face with warmth and love? The sun is not only splendid. It's strong, bold, beautiful and warm. Its very existence and how it rises and set is a beautiful sight.

In light of this, I want you to compare the sun with your passions, hobbies or the things you love doing that light up your world. Bask in those things and create time to enjoy them. You will realize how they help relieve stress and make you a warmer person.

Toxic Free Zone

Butterflies are such dainty creatures. They do have short lifespans, after all. Because of this, pesticides and toxins are poisonous and can kill a butterfly.

Ensure that the area selected for your butterfly garden is pesticide free to ensure you do not harm them. A safe space ensures healthy reproduction of butterflies and a safe haven for these visitors.

Vices *(unhealthy behaviours and addictions)* are a poison that eventually kills you. Sometimes, you may think that you don't engage in them a lot, but that doesn't negate the harm they can bring to you and your loved ones. Have the courage to work on giving them up so you can complete your metamorphosis process.

Some of us may have stagnated at a particular phase of

our lives because we have let our vices take the wheel of our lives. Don't allow yourself to be a slave of sin. Ask God to help you break free. According to 2 Corinthians 10:3-4, our battles are not physical but spiritual.

The Scripture reads, "For though we walk in the flesh, we do not war according to the flesh, for the weapons of our warfare are not of the flesh, but divinely powerful for the destruction of fortresses."

Let prayer be a weapon to help you overcome and win your battles. We are all familiar with the battles we fight every day. Some we conquer day by day, others we are unsure whether we are winning or losing. Some of us fight with our fists, others with our minds, while other battles are fought with prayers while on our knees.

In most of these instances, a cocoon may be involved. We may be in a cocoon of isolation where we feel trapped by our addictions, sin, diseases, depression or financial distress so much that we feel like there is no way out because the darkness has overcome the light of hope that was there.

Some can be tempted to take away their lives or give into hopelessness. I constantly remind myself every day that cocoons are also the same places caterpillars dwell to grow their wings. It's the crucial part of its transformation.

Every moment a butterfly struggles to break free from

its cocoon, that process helps strengthen its muscles. Let these cocoon moments build you. Don't allow those moments to break you.

You are stronger than you know.

Let Peace Reign

As you create that safe space for the butterfly, work on maintaining a peaceful place for them. One that has no loud sounds. You will be surprised by how beautiful peaceful homes attract beautiful beings.

Peaceful environments are safe havens. Where is that mental and physical peace that you desire? Make it your priority to create one because without that peace, you will always struggle to balance your life.

Sometimes, your personality may betray you. I have come to learn the hard way about this. Being an empath, you would always find me helping others and giving away parts of me to make others comfortable and happy at the expense of my peace.

Most of the time, the ones you step in for may never

really appreciate it or even notice you doing so. These days, I guard my peace. Invest in friendships or relationships that give you positive energy as opposed to negative energy.

Don't get me wrong, caring for others is a noble virtue. Do it without destroying yourself in the process. Make a proactive decision about the people you have intertwined your life from your partner to colleagues and even friends.

Your life, inner thoughts and the people around you will either make you a flourishing garden or a place of chaos. If things are not how you wish them to be, you have the power and freedom to change it. Don't allow yourself to be a prisoner of your situations and circumstances.

Weed it accordingly. You owe it to yourself to thrive.

One More Thing

One of my favourite stories that I have come across is about two great friends. One, the sun, was considered magnificent, and the other, a butterfly, very feeble. From high above the sky, they could look at humans living their lives.

The sun boasted about its gift to warm the entire planet and half the time the butterfly didn't know what to boast about. One day, it dawned on the butterfly that its transformation from a caterpillar into a butterfly is a rewarding gift. As it observed humans, it noticed how frail and how many people used to give up unaware that they have more than one chance to transform into something better.

So the butterfly went to the sun and told the sun, *"They can't stop talking about my transformation. I can only do it once in my lifetime. If only they knew, they can do it at any time and in countless ways."*

It is a sad reality that most humans do not realize that transformation is the most grand and most liberating gift. Caterpillar moments can become butterfly moments.

The question is, now that you know this, what's your next move? Do you have the courage it takes to kickstart a hurricane and take your life to the next best level?

Hide me in your arms, Lord,
until the sun comes up and engulfs the darkness.
Don't let me disappear into nothing.
Let me evolve into something.
Let that something be a better version of me.
A wild butterfly.

Help me be bold, fearless, strong,
gentle, graceful, and beautiful all at once.
Make me a wild butterfly that will fly
and spread your love all around the world
for your glory.
As I flap my wings, may I propel change
across the globe and remind all
of your unconditional love.
The love that has defined who I am as your child.

Whenever I get lost,
bring me back to your arms.
When I am brave to fly,
strengthen and guide me
in all my adventures.

About The Author

"Life is beautiful. Step out barefoot, lift up your head and feel the warmth of the sun on your face and feet."

Naomi Wayua Nyamai loves life and believes that everyone needs to embrace the seasons life offer in order to evolve into a Wild Butterfly—the most real version of yourself that you need to discover and grow into.

She is also passionate about children, women, the youth, mental health and environmental conservation. Naomi is a Communication, Brand and Marketing specialist who is currently a PhD candidate and also a youth mentor.